THE BEAUTY
OF MYSTERY

THE BEAUTY
OF MYSTERY

Dorian Grey

To order additional copies of this book, contact:
Xlibris
1-888-795-4274
www.Xlibris.com
Orders@Xlibris.com
714286

CONTENTS

BODY OF WASTE

The desloate desert sounds inviting
to become lost and never found
To forget or roam cursed and beaten down
To hang the balance with his own noose
with laws of attraction acting as the executioner

To feel the hatred of life
and burn the soul to the bone, Cut the vein wide open
and bleed the life from this prison
from This prison I seek revenage

It's not for the reckoning I call you a liar, the theif or whore
I call you that cause I want death

I want death
I want death to come for me
I want death to comfort me

With the gate locked and chained up
With Suicide as the key tied around my neck as I hang
Swinging and swaying in the wind and the rain
To finally die, becoming free from this mortal hell
This fragile useless body and mind

It's not for the reckoning I call you a Liar, The Theif or Whore
I call you that cause I want death

I want death

I want death to come for me

I want death to comfort me

To have this restless soul unbound from these shackless of inhumanity

I want to bleed for days

To burn at the steak

To chomp at the bit, no more

To never want love again

TO be left in perfect darkness

Can i watch the angels and demons fall to the bottomless pit?

TO die is to be free

And to be free is to end this by my own right hand

There will be no better times, unless you hang me high

Sorrow is mine to enjoy

or hate in that I have not made my desicion

Yet I long for the worms to taste my lefeless flesh

For atleast they will find enjoyment out of this body of waste

DEVIL'S LOST LOVE

He asked me to write about something that can't find him out

Do people wanted to hear what I said?

Am I just a crazy?

or do I have a spoken secert to share?

Come find out and see the enigma

The smoke screen of sharp words and doubled edged daggers into the back of the young

I watched her tongue turn firehyrdent red

As her thoart dried up and she choked onto the words she heard in her head

"Can I hide from this" she sprays out towards the onlooking people

"Where are you looking?" she snapped out

The sky is faded to dusk and the cigarette smoke fills the lasting light

with blue accented film

In forgien body langauge he strolled over to her

Asking where see found heaven?

Where does the devil search for the dead?

Where will the dead find Death?

She said "I can only see into the piano, that the devil plays,

"Once in a full moon he'll sit and play a sonnet, an ode to his lost love

"His broken fingers scratch the ivory, His broken fingers scratch the ivory!!"

"Thank you, for a reason to listen to the full moon sing" He spoke through a haze of cigarette smoke

As he turn to leave and walk into the night

Whislting the tune of the devils lost love

ADDICTION

The addiction snares at the door

Prown and ready to shot through the veins of an already broken soul

A skeleton thrown from the closet and laid sprawled out on the couch

mind wondering

sleep deprived until you say "yes"

(a very sorry and solemn yes)

To a haunting, taunting time from the previous sins of an old life

Chaos and Strife

The silver lining went dark

Till you locked the poison vice into a coffin

Nailed and crucified like christ

Bled dry into the ground from which this addiction grow and turned into hells messenger

The devil has his right hand full of victims

and his left hand holds the vile, needle and powder to which they will be slaves to

This bless'd bastard addiction

A perfect depiction of failure and loss

After this debt will be paid in full cost

And still this addiction snares at the door

Longing for you to need more

Lingering Lamp

This lingering lamp

Light encased in shadows

Yet to the core it stays brightier (like those eyes)

The light house opens to the eye of the strom

Still we can't figure if it's going to be a rocky grave or sandy
paradise

(to where they lay)

With the crashing of 2 matters

(bodies created for eachother)

The Pulling and Pushing of Gaining or of Losing something

With the moon pulling the tide out towards its gaze

So will the night reveal all that's under the sun, under the
scars and graves

As the sun rises the tide

It also rasies interest to what the moon brings

Creating a scene of "What Ifs" to be understood or Misunderstood

(depending on where she lays)

And still the lingering lamp shows all I remembered from the sun

(that morning smile)

Also getting to indugle with the freedom of what the moon
will bring

(her silhouette)

How I Miss

How I miss her body laid under sheets
I'm eagerly waiting for the next moment to be on top of her

Fingers and lips touch and feel
The shock of loving so tightly heals

Show me the meaning of this
Show me you naked and my bliss
Show me where on you, I should kiss

Eyes darkened by passion, Scorned by sinners lust
Scenes so beautiful they creep out of the walls
Yet they wont tell a soul of the burlesque movie
They have just experienced
Witness to my eyes and Witness to my love
I can't bear this until Im alone

Walk down town to see the seashore and the bodies it spits up
Walk down town to see my bed and the mermaid I strung
across it

How I miss her
How can I beat this
Heart and Hand
and knife sliding down my back
How I miss this

BURN

The cocaine doesn't burn anymore

My nose burns but for your scent

Only to have you run through my viens

My heart attack pains will be your gain in the intoxicating evening

As you stop my vitals

Events shattered from the image

Drugs resist, and Love kills this high

Cause I'll fly close to the sun for you

I'll cusre my very exsitence for you

I'll dry my cries for you

I'll be your....... Your Atlantis

Nights turn to poison, Now that it's been over and done

Closure burns into my wrist just as the blade, I held so close for 2 yrs

Cut through all my nerves

To never feel.....Be my curse or Be my blessing?

To always be cold

To always be dead

To be walking, emotions died the day the sun covered my bed

Since you where gone with the night

Laws of Attraction

There happens to be miracles in every moment of every scene
Even after time stops and timespace continues
Love blossoms into stars, Moons and Planets
Not knowing what happens to miracles
Articles upon articles
Piled up past the sky
Past the milky way to find God

Is love just God?
Since love is not an emotion and God doesn't exist in emotion
Does love and God = the same plan?

Are laws meant to be broken?
or just futrue guide lines to question all in life, love and faith?
Pulling or Pushing us onwards, downwards, upwards, left or
right towards the same cross roads?

Young or old, can love keep us tied together
(Only if we get over ourselves)
and relieze that (love) is not an emotion
but a powerful constant that makes timespace look useless

Nothing has Changed

I awake to find nothing has changed
Nothing has come of these sleepless nightmare filled dreams

The night is still young, old or maybe just cold

Does this all make sense?
Will it all fit into this box or sphere?

I awake to a shadow looking for a place to warm his hand
Unexplained and decent
I start a fire and pour some coffee
And enjoy the old yet fresh company of the shadow

Covered in Black, Painted red eyes
with compassion as masscare
The shadow sips at his coffee and falls into the trance of the fire
No questions, No words, No thoughts have been exercised
Silence needed to be heard

Dreams, Nightmares or just Mind Games
I sit and enjoy the company

I awake and find nothing has changed
Nothing has Changed

I TO BE CURSED

I, to be cursed
To walk as the living and never to feel death
Even after the gallows have hung me high

This I write not to be known but to make it known
The path I have ventured is not a path of victories
Yet I don't wish to distract you with these words
This path leads to rich's and profond living (only in the after life)

The way you walk is poisoned and lonely
Still I ventured it to seek a higher searching and higher love
Take heed, this path will lead you to hell and heaven spitting
you out

Do as your heart says but have your soul light the way from
day to day
Make no mistake you will encounter a curse and hold it dear
Hold it close and don't let it consume you but let it drive you
towards Davey Jones locker

FRAYED

I remember walking across a chasam.

My heart beating chaoiticly, faster then I can walk

Hanging over the chasam, A rope bridge hanging in the still stale air

No movment, No noise

I can only hear such a loud, dishearting voice not an echo but the fear of falling

Closer to the bridge I stand Now seeing the ropes of the bridge fray

The planks of wood cracked and splintered

but this is the path I need to take

The one that could kill me

Pushing me to a new razors edge

One foot reaches for the first plank

The crack, that sound off, Was the same scream that you hear when a siren gets her heart stolen

Forward I march, Down the Haggered bridge.......

PAST

They never grow stronger
They just grow older
Temptation never reach my heart

With the watch tower, Fading out
The shores of strange lands, Thin out
Still the Captin stands on the crows nest
With no sins on his hands
With no purple heart on his vest

You must
Find the path that is best for you
Find the thorns carrying the prove
Not the show, Not to see, But to tell

A gigantic place to be
Staring out at sea
With the shore against the castle walls
confined in these stone halls
Pictures of the heretic dead
Long satin to sheet the kings bed

A dimished home stead
Burned down to ashe
but regined supereme all through the past

Mystical Angel

An Angel or A Mystical lover of lost souls

Yet one night has become all the dreams we dream

and all the lips whisper are mused by her lips and what she
has spoken

The eyes crawling upon the face that look into them

Knowing that maybe this could be it

Knowing that this might be over

Something from this angel will end something

Ending something that has been holding you chained and
beated down

She will end the fear that holds us here

Even if you coward out

She will fight for you to be what you fear the most

She will bring the shadows around you

So you can finally see with Your Heart, Your Soul

and forget about Your Eyes and Mind

A Vision in May

A man can only hate
As long as he looks to the mirror for answers

I will drink the poison to enjoy you in my fleeting moments
before I go
My body will decay but my soul will haunt your heart forever

A cocktail for a lasting love
Your kiss chased by my poison

So my eye will have you for my last Vision in May

An elegant liquid to have slide down my throat
into my veins
Through my heart to concrete our brave love
with one last kiss
I will never say "goodbye"
The love we made into reality will never die
Time will be fleeting
but the love I gave you will never have a fleeting day

YOU ARE MY LAST VISION IN MAY

Left to Right or Right to Wrong

Coffins held in a row
under where we walk, friend or foe?

This, we will never know
until we find heaven or hell
Saints or Sinners

As we decide the longivity of where we stay for eterinty
Blessed are those who seek mystery and hide from knowledge
Looking for what not to see, and still knowing all that happened
Hell may have our names but Heaven is as cusred as the earth

Cursed to fight the ground
and told never to ask questions.... of WHY

Foot prints in the sand and snow
Left to right or right to wrong
With the man at the gate and ghost locked under cage
and the Angels watching from heaven

IMMORTALITY

I've been stripped of this for so long
(meaningless endeavours)
To find the only key/secert of this life
Yet being a mortal is a blessing
And still immortality will hunt/haunt me
(to close for comfort)
All The Gods, The Demons, and The Ttians
All carry my scent, cut into their souls

Once I told the devil my story
I found hell (which I created)
In the eyes I looked to everyday
(Where the monsters reign)
Immortality please fall from the plank in my eye
and let the devil deal with living and never ending
Mortality please kiss my forehead
Leaving the mark of your sweet kiss of death

I Love to Know that I Don't Know

I love to know that I don't know

Let the ship sail into the fog and leave the mind to wonder in searching and seeking

Yet never to find where they rest and live in peace forever

The blues player that drank the poison and died.

Yet no one knows who he was and where he came from

The devil at the cross roads

With the music and chords that became the corner stone

The myth is the truth and the stories will be the scenes for life

I want to be unknown and unheard of

My grave laid in the dust with no name and no title to be remembered

I love to know that I don't know

IMAGINE

Deserts roam this earth
Hidden in sand, its always fleeting from thy hand
Dirt, lizards, snakes and ritual birds
Lifeless to the eye

Life living into reality
Lizards, snakes and ritual birds
All Daring enough to fly
Rigorous to the night, fullfilling to the fight

Locked up into a solid
Break it, Smash it, Burn it, You will never endure it
You must eat what the surface gives
Drink what the plant of throns leak to the surface

Imagine, Not what lies beneath
Curiosity kills the koolest kat
Suit and all
To become Naked, swirling, deteriorate into Art

CURSED OR BOLD

Which card is yours?
Death, The Theif, or The Joker on High?

Death will be met with a sweet kiss on my lips
and her face will never be seen or gazed upon

The Thief stole the cornerstone right from under the nose of
the king
Leaving drops of blood as a trail to where the ram was
murdered

The Joker on high fabled to be the king of hearts with suicide
by his side
and a laugh like the sirens sorrowful love song
To lull you to sleep and sit on the throne

Which card is yours to hold?
Are you Cursed or Are you Bold?

CRAWL BACK TO ME

Crawl back to me
Enter the mirror and stand in front of the curtains
Until I say cut

Then dance like no one is watching
Fading out the scene, we'll stop and the curtain will drop

Your naked and just standing in time
with the beat of the drum echoing the beat of your heart

Your feet start to tap
Tip toe across the floor like your gliding on a cloud
Tip toeing through the tulips to hide in the shroud
Of blood you left as you broke the mirror I stood you in front of

Crawl back to me
Crawl back to me

ENIGMA

Is it the checmicals that hold the enigma or the key?

Will this porch cover me from the rain
and shadow me from the sun?

The rose has faded to grey, turning into an enigma to the wrold
(never to be seen in pure beauty)

Orgainzed chaos to distract you from the truth
The truth of the matter will stay hidden
In the blurred form, in the trenchs dug into the viens

But I still don't want to leave this shadow of pure beauty
The shadow of cold conspiracy
The shadow of overloaded Capacity

A Long Time Coming

Now it's been a long time coming
Waiting for this shadow to lift off this broken heart
Coughing up black tar inbetween yellow teeth
It reigns closer, closer then the moon and sun as twins
and still all I see is a reflection of eyes in the blackened mirror
bound together by needles and daggers
Finger prints and Selfish ignorence towards this palace

Please catch for us the foxes that stomp through these grounds
In selfish longning
Hidden under the shadows
From the shade of the sun

PAID THE FEE

Set free
Paid the ultimate fee
To watch the sky collide into your eye
and now the shadows won't cease from haunting me

With the enigma in plain sight

Im scared in a whirl wind fright

In the eye of the storm, Starving yet still alive enough to fight
this off
To stay alive insight and free from these nightmareish dreams
Silhouettes and Stellatos walk this floor
In search for so much more, for so much more

Even after I paid the fee, found no key
Never to walk free

Dorian Grey

ETC ETC ETC

Coughing, Clawing through the rabbit hole
The whole of the world is flat
Calmly we walk off the edge and fall through the universe
Torn by a black hole

Space is not the final frontier
to look deeper is to dive into darkness (the rabbit hole)
Are we late?
Is time truly relevant?

Coughing, Awoken under water and stars roam around the
blurry lines
Still no light is shimmering
Sputtering past the cracks
Down the walls, into the halls
and Onwards to Etc, Etc, Etc

6 Sense

There is some sort of twinkle in her eyes
I've never seen before
Crossing over my mind I want to feel more
Crossing the 7 seas and never did I see
such lust and lore

To seize my soul and experience
in so much more (than 6 senses)

No more wanting sierns and whores
To lay with her forever and unveil the mystery
of what I can't or shouldn't see
Cutting to the core and lingering

For never will she be a bore
(to the heart strings soar)

GRAVITY

The strength

The wind through the trees

Earth spinning

Undertoe pulling

Under the unknown force

Through the problem and cause

The strength

Rambles on, Humbly and Bumbly down, down, down towards the trees

It's all aches from growing pains

From experience and faulty planning

or maybe it's all prudent to the bone

Peeling back the flesh, For the skin hides the bone

Carving through the bone to find the marrow, In which we need to suck from life

ABSORBED

The image absorbed like water to bread
Until it becomes to heavy to tread the surface
Sinking to the bottom of the grimey deep
Whats the purpose?

In the painting of the sun
The colours blend
All is done and falls to the horizions introduction

Am I Alive?
Did I dream in this watery scheme?
Vivid Imagrey stirs the fliud of the mind
Am I Alive?
Are the stars real?
Has all been Absorbed?
Have all been Absorbed?
How is all this Absorbed?

Or Will We

The sound we made
Is the sound played
and to never be heard again

The noise that the shadows heed
The mega feeling of this palace mead
Signal the forth coming of the new love of life and her lover
but we still dont know who's who
Is life the lover and death the mistress or
Is the flipped room the mirrors truth

Will death be the lover and life the mistress?

We will find all this out in the next circle, or will we?

Dirt and Graves

The Hanging of the so called "men"

These creatures that longed to be "Gods"

And yet only sold their souls to the dirt and grime

Can these ropes truly hang the recokoning we're all watching for?

Well our daggers find the veins to bleed these nightmares dry?

Dropping into the depths of these dreams

The music, the Plot, All the scenery of heavens and hells

Simply forced together by the chains we have linked through our hearts and graves

I Knew I Knew

I knew, I knew

> But I tried to close the door on knowing
> With a window open the door closes
> Quicker then zens right hand showing why peace reigns

> Fresh air becokons for an open door
> Ignorence bleeds like a leech's dinner

I knew, I knew

> Where the birds fly
> with their feather malting and drifting to the north of hell
> So where will hell lay?
> Why is hell the mystery to souls?

Forsaken Hope

Light the match and see how the nightmares scatter and shutter down the cracks in the floor

Trying to never be seen

Yet found lying under the bed with the monsters and thoughts so frightening

God can't even speak thier names

Forsaken hope?

Maybe this is just a part of being human?

Our minds are calling cards for sin

Our minds are just the perfect poison

Leaking into our viens

Dripping from our tongues for all to taste

BROKEN BOTTLES

Broken bottles

Forgotten dreams

To be drowned infront of the public

And still, They dont acknowlegde it died

Pints take a breath to enjoy and still I cannot summon a whipser of air

Speak her name

Her Lips Silky, Red, and a poison so refined

Its the perfect way to die

Casterted by one glance and a wink

To find everything in her eyes

All from broken bottles

Maybe we can drown the dead, and never forget the dream

12 Steps

The scurutiny of the bottle is a 12 step program

The enigma to the hallow grave will be maggots and pentagrams

With this I creep along life on egg shells
Tip Toeing towards the noose and freedom

Taste, Smell and See
The dark horse
lead by the hell hounds and the darkest force
Hell Bound
As Heaven left me in the gutter'd hearse
Have I fallen to the ground?
Only to enjoy maggots and the 12 steps to the bottle?

OF THE WORLD

Why does he write when he sees me every day of the world?

Can't he remember why I love him?
His broken hand writing shows the mystery of love
and so last forever, my soul and how I longed for him

The description of me, he so wrote neatly
Yet with every crossed out "mistake"
It shows the imperfections from above

Although he writes me every day of the world
I love to read what I mean to him every minute of the world

LOVER MISTRESS

Suicide notes float on the bed
Like rose pedals I placed when I first fell in love with her
That was on a spring early morning
We kissed as soon as I awoke, with a gasp of oxygen
And I was hers and She was mine
(My Lover)

One afternoon I fell into her
To rebel in the lust of what I can never have
That snowy afternoon she stole my breath
As we kissed
I long to have her, She owns me eternally
(My Mistress)

HONESTY

This book is not here to defraud the mystery
These shadows, This enigma is real
It walks amougest the wild things
It will have the will to finish
Yet it bleeds not and will not dimish
and haunt these hallow grounds we fight for

It becomes it's own monster, It's own hero
Amoung the moon and sun

Not yet convinced of its honesty?

This is not a fable or tale
Layed promptly on the table
To never close the veil

ORGANIZED

"Unless we orgainze we are lost"
said the man with no spare time for wonder
Coffee, cigerettes and trusting time itself
to produce some sort of structured ceremony

Blessed are the meek and the strong willed man
who laughs at mystery and "NO" is spoken to the harlot
in whispered tones of grace

Mystery is the structure, Mystery is fun to wonder to and
from
Yet mystery is the curse of organized not knowing

PRESENCE TO PRESENT

A Goddess honours my pressence
Her whispers still linger on my ear drum
I can still taste the words "Enjoy my curves"

Dancing dirty
Lace and silk all over my skin
Yet I still haven't seen her face,
Enjoyed the windows to her soul

The Harlot of darkness
The Princess of mystery
My siern to sing the song of seduction
As my lulliby

A Goddess Honoured to be my present

Gods are in the Clouds

The Gods are in the clouds
Well so they say

We must be crazy to believe in a sense of more then 6
More then all we can imgaine

We praise something that will never grace or curse this earth
For a Gain
We struggle, They breed the lies maybe the truth
They play the enigma
They play the veins of the heros and victims
To secure their faces, So they will never be seen

RESTLESS

It's restless
Im restless
The spirit is crying to be tamed or free'd
And still the lost are damned or captured

All these photo albums of this so far, so failed life

Restless and lost
Never confused or willing to linger alone
From those you retain a vision of confidence
This restless sense is a curse with a love for more
With hatred towards finding out what lies beneath

Martyr or Fool

Covered in blood

Covered by a white cloth

The man who gave it all will be a mystery (the unknown martyr)

and yet the man who talked and never gave (The fool)

will be long lived by all

The unknown will be burned to ash

The known will stand immortal for all to see

How does comfort breed heros?

When the solider died in battle

and the coward hid in gravel?

Proof on the Pudding Skin

The time spent waiting

is the time you spent play over in your mind

What lies under/within the shadows

Mystery of a dectetive is the primary function of the scene of the crime

Clues to find the truth in the pudding

Is the skin of the proof

Left hanging from the teeth of the innocent

Blue prints, Foot prints, Finger prints

Left in the time we spend waiting

END

Let me speak in tongues

and conjour up something unfamilar, unfamable to actully speak of

Even in a whisper ears will burn

Cities will fall to their knees

This cornerstone is nothing more then a spirit and folklore

Created to never be questioned or answered in a dream

Pierced to the core

Left to die and more

Will we see this to the end?

Dorian Grey

HOME

Do we really know how it ends?
Can we dicitate faith or the progress of souls
To belief in heaven nor hell?

Mystery is the path we walk
Mysteries are the compass to more
Guide us "HOME"
To a place where we belong

Don't show me the wrong
Don't make it feel right
Just make it "HOME" for tonight
and don't let me know the fright

Forget the Sun

Is it the diamond or the coal?
Finding out that we have a goal
We broke in
Stole the night
From the moon and the sun's shadowy path
With a fork in the road
We ate our pinic in limbo

The diamond is the only thing to cut through the truth
With the coal sustaining the fire
To shadow the night
Forget the sun

LIMBO

Im not close
Im not far
Im stuck in limbo

It's a fair farce
To have hell as my creation and the tale to keep me alive
Please stay here
Far from you my dear, Till your eyes find mine
I'll stay hidden in the scrutiny of hell
Let the door bell ring to the locked door

And be stuck in Limbo

E, E, E

Entangled, Released (as a soft opening)
Poeple crowd around
The doors blackened and only one way viewing
(So the show is unknown)
Entraced by the dakrness and silhouettes (to be found out)
Ensnared by Ignorence and bliss of the unknowning

Do the stars come out to play?

DEATH AND SEX

Death and Sex are entangled
in this broken mirror we call life

Choke me
Break me
Make me
Let me
Fall from your tongue

Death and Sex
entangled in the bed sheets of our ecsatcy and apparitions
Cut me
Break me to fall to my knees
In love for you

HYDRATE

Why does the water hydrate?
Is the science excate or is the belief in sweet relief real?

Sitting by the creek
Soothing the soul, Yet death drowns the young in faster days
All to see who really loves life's mystery

LONG BEFORE

He's world vanished
Long before
He appeared
Casting out a single time
As the frame work he managed vainished

EASIER

It is easier to hate than to love
It is easier to fear than to be couragious

Or Will We

The sound we made
Is the sound played
and to never be heard again

The noise that the shadows heed
The mega feeling of this palace mead
Signal the forth coming of the new love of life and her lover
but we still dont know who's who
Is life the lover and death the mistress or
Is the flipped room the mirrors truth

Will death be the lover and life the mistress?

We will find all this out in the next circle, or will we?

Sands of Time

Im going to the opera of life
Take a slice with my knife
From the back of the sly
String him up and not let him die

Shall a ghost tell the truth?
The grave will show the prove
Listen to the rain pound of the roof
See the 4 deadly horsemens hoof

Held in the sand of time

In a conscience hand
Sing and dance in line
Place the dead where they kicked the can
Write a note and hang it out on the politicans stand

Sex, Pleasure and Truth

The silhouette of enigma
Silent night, Oh holy night
Filled with sin and lust

Broke my crown, left tried and dyed
with the scent of love, hate and passions

SEX... Mysterious feelings, A human experience finding what
fits and feels exciting and dangorous

Pleasure... Eyes locked, seeking for writtings of lust inbetween
the lines of the pupils
Tracing pictures from the scars of the past

TRUTH... The point of the sphinx handling the light,
spotting the blemishing skin and crows feet
Yet we'll still enjoy SEX and PLEASURE with the angels
watching

SIERNS SONG

I've been searching

To this place I write the left over by my write hand
holding a mouth full of sand

Dancing flames across the battle field
The men I left scattered and dead
My right hand had left the battle to embrace
A Sierns Song

SLIGHT OF HAND

With a slight of hand

I'll be on my way

Pay the man and ask if this is his card

Tuxedo with tails flowing in the wind

Still the colour is not there

Then in a split second

A message comes across the wire

Someone calling for my hand, but she gave her hand to someone else

That's why Im in New York

Streets filled with broken dreams, Still having hope to glue them together

Gutters filled with trash

Curbs laid with winos and newspaper sheets

The same scene I grow up in

Dead yet beating the drum

Laughing yet tears carry out the scene

Is this an escape?

or just a change of fasle escape?

Im still chained to he city

Im still bound to her lips

Im still holding hope of dead dreams

With a slight of hand

I'll start a new life or is it a change of scene?

Feeling the same, Girls stay the same, Just different names

I can't break the model

I exhaust the model over, over and over again

I call them by the same name

but still enjoy different palaces with these ladies

In my mind twins from the last heir

all twins with the same sin

I enjoy

Will I break this cycle?

Change everything I know, Everything I call life?

That is for god to see

but not for him to decide for me

Free will, will burn

Dictator will yern for unbinding speechs

SOULFULL

The knife in your back
Is the dagger in my hand
It will be easier to let it stand

I'm the devils only son
Broken, beaten, souless and paid for in full
I do Appoligize for my attiude
I'm Broken, Beaten and lost a game of liars dice

My Heart is still mine
But never will it be without a hole

The knife in your back
Is held in my left hand
But the dagger in my right hand
Has slit the devils throat

A Soul for A soul
A Soul for A Soul
A Soulfull for A soul

SPACE SILHOUETTES

Silhouettes

What will they look like?
Will it resemble the blue moon
Wolves hollowing for the nights touch
Will I be forever young, like Dorian Gray?
(silent, still, locked in a frame)

My Doom, Your fear of the night
Your Doom, My fear of never seeing my reflection

City lights
Block all the light to the dark space
Black holes, Planets collide
Dreams and fictional murders
There are no reflections, No Silhouettes to be seen

Forever midnight
Forever midnight

Space is doom Incarnate

Dorian Grey

STEP

A step away from the light

Is a step, Maybe a step to far

The door is closed

The lights are off

Just one candle is dancing, flickering in the middle of the room

Strippers Real Name

Into a darkroom
Lights dimmed, stars glow on the celling
Lights flicker on the stage top

The Dj introduces the next performer
LIGHTS, SMOKE and heres Destiny
Legs long and lushes
Accentuated by Stilettos and Lace

As she dances with herself
To keep hidden her real name
The lights dim to intensify her silhouette
With no shame, It's all a game

The art of seduction
The art of Curves
The art of sex
The Mystery of the strippers real name

STYLE AND EDITION

The devil

        Has a library filled with 1 book

        Cast and printed in the style and edition you could

think in

Jesus carries

        Paper notes, hymns, and all you can think in

        Cast and printed in the style and edition of

1 book

So who drew the line in the sand?

Spoke in tongues

Cast out spirits

and raped the innocent

        Never to think of freedom

        Never to believe in the eternal more

TASTE

Light the match and see how the nightmares scatter

Shatter down to the cracks in the floor

Never to be scene

and found lieing under the bed with our monsters and thoughts

That we swept under the rug

God cannot even speak their names or gaze upon their pressence

Forsaken Hope?

or Maybe just a part of being human?

Our minds are counting cards of sin

Our minds are just the perfect poison

Leaking into our viens

Dripping from our tongues

All for a taste

THE BEAUTY OF MYSTERY

Crawling down the walls
under the carpet and across the halls

Have you seen this before?
or Is it a dream of somthing more?

Screams preceed to fall on sleeping ears
Fanit shadows in the elegant lights
Strangers or Friends
Alleys to a dead end?

The question to still be answered
The Beauty of Mystery

Why will the night become colder
Will shadows roam the plains?
Will they be seen by all eyes
or Just the eyes of the innocent to the dark horror?

The Jurys Out

Standing at the cross roads
Switch blade in hand
Right hand bloody
Left hand broken and clutching the devils tail
Caught him in the twist of lies
with a bear trap I feed 10 thousand mouths with white smoke
and black lungs filled with the devils noise

and still the jury's out

The light at the end of the road is owned by noone
and I still linger on her tongue to be left behind

THE POISON, THE GUN, THE NOOSE AND THE GRAVE

The man in the mirror

hides a secret upon which

No human will see

The Poison, The Gun, The Noose and The Grave

will hold the secrets safe in warm bodies of the worms

The Poison will hinder thy Breathe

The Gun leaves fear behind

The Noose hangs the sin

The Grave is the door way to freedom

To finally see the answer to the Beauty of Mystery

Understanding that once the worms taste us they hold our secrets

The beauty of it is that we will only understand it all

after the game is done and we are all bought out

THE STATUE

A Broken, Bleeding eye of the needle
A strong sunny day at the steeple
with weak and willing people

All shufflinig Straight Forward
In Hallways and Core doors

A gross amount of fliud
Spews out
from this water way of this statue
Flowing knee deep past you
and beyond the inner circle
Spheres, Squares, Pyrmaids and Pentagrams
In linear lines
In ryhthmic times
Chained, To be binds of reality
A candle in the wind
Dust settling at the cross roads
Where you left your kins bloody knee prints
After your last drug stint

THE STRANGER
AND THE MOON

Down the gutter road
with the open moon dancing with the stranger
Down the field was thrown
with the stranger catching the moon
Down to the place?
People ask the stranger
Smiling back at your face?
People ask the moon
Can we see the ivory tower and the ebony man
Dancing as the stranger and the moon

The crow ran away with the spoon
and the fork jumped to the moon
As the stranger waltzed to the beat all night
The stranger and the moon stayed in each others sight

Can you watch this day pass by
A plank in the eye is worst then sty
and still we look to the sky
and seek answers from the moon
As the stranger stands in the shadows
Dancing with the spoon
The demons hallow and growl to hate the night
After the moon stands to watch
The stranger mocks the blessed sight
Still the stranger dances with the moon
and it will end so soon
As it started in such a fury
Get all those veins dry in a hurry

THE STRANGER

Covered in rain and as the fog enhances The Stranger

Trench coat and cane

Walking in the midnight hour

Looking for something that noone has seen or heard of being found

Alley ways have become the Ivory palace to The Stranger

People are warned yet have never met

This mystery, This enigma of something we imagined up?

Is this Jack the Ripper

Is this Davy Jones

Is this the Invisible man

Is this Dorian Gray

Is this Dr Jekyll or Mr Hyde

All just with an elegant languor

Is this the man that haunts your dreams

and becomes just a faded picture of what was to come

As The Stranger walks dusk to dusk and dust to hell

The Stranger will Always be The Stranger

The Truth of the Legends

The Rain is the tears of the Gods
(well so they say)
How can the Gods feel pain
When all they now is Gain ?

Well maybe they have realized that all the feeble (fable) gain
is to live in Heaven or Hell

Earth is still an enigma to their minds and soul
and still they have never touched the ground with their soles
Could they be the lost souls?
Ghost, Gods and the Immortals?

As we are The living, The dying, The truth of the legends

TO THE END

Let me speak in tongues?

Let me conjour up something unfamilar, unfamthable, To never actully speak of

Never in a whisper, Ears will burn

Cities will fall to their knees

This cornerstone is nothing more then a spirit or folklore

Crearted to never be questioned or answered in a dream

Piereced to the core

Left to die no more

Will we see this to the end?

VAIL

It becomes it's own monster

It's own hero

Not yet convinced of it honesty

This is not a Fable or Tale

Laid promptly on the table

For us to never close or reveal whats behind the vail

WATCH

Watch.......

        The Mother Breed

        The Father PLead

        The Sister Bleed

        and The Son Feed

Into the Earth that spins

Intwined in the chords of space

Inbetween the chords of losing face

The Center of the Universe

Omni-present

A mouthy peasant lurking in mud

Hands stained with red Blood

Just watch........

        It will never cease spinning

Way Out There

What a weirdo
To view things in the dark
Absent of light No fright towards alonely night
All to View things
Through bay windows
Spinster widows, petting cats, Chasing birds
Like old bards chasing words

Way out there, amoungest the tulips
NO throns grow
No leaves blow
No fireflies glow.......Way out there

The steam rises from the waters
The dew drips from the lilies
The frogs sing with the doves
All can be heard and seen from.... Way out there

Widows and Door

Only if you follow

The door will be perceived as open

The windows closed and boarded up

Lights dimed to set the mood

with a hint of candle light lingering in the sky

Darkness will fall and hide nothing from the touch

Window

Misery Love company
Misery is my only company

Turned my back on the Devil
Drank wine with Jesus

The dagger in my back
was stabbed there by my Left hand
Looking over my Right shoulder
No excuses, only Possession

Bruning Bridges is much easier then counting toys
Sitting at the window, watching the rain fall all around
Watching the tree roots reach for the skies
But fall to the ground
The wind doesn't make a sound
Buy a round for all the chaps who are glory bound

Dorian Grey

WOUNDED SHADOWS

I'll be keeping those shadows wounded
hidden in the dark, Im your worst nightmare
In the hollows of this tomb, a candle lite and floating
with a sliver bullet covered in blood.
Is this a lie, The cliff hanger, The inscrutable death of this all

Why can't you see this, The pain your healing or causeing
Throw a match and light up this tomb
Keep these shadows fleeting and wounded
Keep those shadows fleeting and wounded

With a smile of insecurity
and a helping hand to die
I'll keep these shadows wounded
Under the light of the blood red sky
Under the moon you'll see this shadows wounded

You Got Us Here

You got us here
and now we've left
You Can't control the lights and sounds of the masscared

The ball has started
The room has filled with smoke
and the first note has been received

You got us dead
and now we're here
Leaving this ballad to starve
Note for Note, Line for line and a song for the flesh of the desired